W9-BRU-235

Eaglets

by Anne Wendorff

BELLWETHER MEDIA · MINNEAPOLIS, MN

BLASTOFF! READERS

Note to Librarians, Teachers, and Parents:

Blastoff! Readers are carefully developed by literacy experts and combine standards-based content with developmentally appropriate text.

Level 1 provides the most support through repetition of high-frequency words, light text, predictable sentence patterns, and strong visual support.

Level 2 offers early readers a bit more challenge through varied simple sentences, increased text load, and less repetition of high-frequency words.

Level 3 advances early-fluent readers toward fluency through increased text and concept load, less reliance on visuals, longer sentences, and more literary language.

Level 4 builds reading stamina by providing more text per page, increased use of punctuation, greater variation in sentence patterns, and increasingly challenging vocabulary.

Level 5 encourages children to move from "learning to read" to "reading to learn" by providing even more text, varied writing styles, and less familiar topics.

Whichever book is right for your reader, Blastoff! Readers are the perfect books to build confidence and encourage a love of reading that will last a lifetime!

This edition first published in 2009 by Bellwether Media, Inc.

No part of this publication may be reproduced in whole or in part without written permission of the publisher. For information regarding permission, write to Bellwether Media, Inc., Attention: Permissions Department, Post Office Box 19349, Minneapolis, MN 55419.

Library of Congress Cataloging-in-Publication Data
Wendorff, Anne.
   Eaglets / by Anne Wendorff.
     p. cm. – (Blastoff! readers. Watch animals grow)
   Includes bibliographical references and index.
   Summary: "A basic introduction to eaglets. Developed by literacy experts with simple text and full color photography for students in kindergarten through third grade"–Provided by publisher.
   ISBN-13: 978-1-60014-239-0 (hardcover : alk. paper)
   ISBN-10: 1-60014-239-7 (hardcover : alk. paper)
   1. Eagles–Infancy–Juvenile literature. I. Title.

QL696.F32W47 2009
598.9'42139–dc22   2008033536

Contents

A mother eagle
lays eggs.
Inside each egg
is an eaglet.

An eaglet must break out of its egg. It pecks a hole with its **egg tooth**.

egg tooth

It can take
two days to
break out of
the egg.

Eaglets chirp for food. The mother and father eagle bring food to the eaglets.

An eaglet is born with fluffy feathers called **down**.

Eaglets grow feathers for flight when they are five to six weeks old.

Eaglets must be careful not to fall from the nest. They do not know how to fly yet.

An eaglet hops to learn how to fly. It flaps its wings in the air.

19

Eaglets that try to fly are called **fledglings**. Soon eaglets are ready to soar!

Glossary

down—soft and fluffy feathers; newborn eaglets are covered in down.

egg tooth—a sharp tooth; an eaglet uses an egg tooth to break out of its egg.

fledgling—an eaglet that is learning to fly

To Learn More

AT THE LIBRARY

Hatcher, Darlene W. *Little Eaglet Loses Her Feathers*. Tulsa, Okla.: Insight Publishing Group, 2002.

Minshull, Evelyn. *Eaglet's World*. Morton Grove, Ill.: Albert Whitman & Company, 2005.

Stearns, Carolyn. *Quiet Please—Eaglets Growing*. Centreville, Md.: Tidewater Publishers, 2002.

ON THE WEB

Learning more about eaglets is as easy as 1, 2, 3.

1. Go to www.factsurfer.com.

2. Enter "eaglets" into the search box.

3. Click the "Surf" button and you will see a list of related Web sites.

With factsurfer.com, finding more information is just a click away.

Index

The images in this book are reproduced through the courtesy of: Jeff Foott / Getty Images, front cover; Ron Niebrugge / Alamy, p. 5; David Gowans / Alamy, p. 7; Arctic-Images / Getty Images, p. 9; Klaus Nigge / Getty Images, p. 11; Art Wolfe / Getty Images, p. 13; Peter Arnold Inc. / Alamy, p. 15; Mira / Alamy, p. 17; Getty Images, p. 19; Randall Ingalls / Alamy, p. 21.